IT'S MY STATE! ★

DELAWARE

David C. King

Brian Fitzgerald

 **Marshall Cavendish**
Benchmark
New York

Other Marshall Cavendish Offices:
Marshall Cavendish International (Asia) Private Limited, 1 New Industrial Road, Singapore 536196 •
Marshall Cavendish International (Thailand) Co Ltd. 253 Asoke, 12th Flr, Sukhumvit 21 Road, Klongtoey Nua,
Wattana, Bangkok 10110, Thailand • Marshall Cavendish (Malaysia) Sdn Bhd, Times Subang, Lot 46, Subang
Hi-Tech Industrial Park, Batu Tiga, 40000 Shah Alam, Selangor Darul Ehsan, Malaysia

Marshall Cavendish is a trademark of Times Publishing Limited

All websites were available and accurate when this book was sent to press.

Library of Congress Cataloging-in-Publication Data
King, David C.
          Delaware / David C. King, Brian Fitzgerald. — 2nd ed.
                p. cm. — (It's my state!)
          Includes index.
          ISBN 978-1-60870-048-6
          1. Delaware—Juvenile literature. I. Fitzgerald, Brian, 1972- II. Title.
     F164.3.K56 2011
     975.1—dc22   2010003920

Second Edition developed for Marshall Cavendish Benchmark by RJF Publishing LLC (www.RJFpublishing.com)
Series Designer, Second Edition: Tammy West/Westgraphix LLC
Editor, Second Edition: Amanda Hudson

All maps, illustrations, and graphics © Marshall Cavendish Corporation. Maps and artwork on pages 6, 40, 41, 75, 76, and back cover by Christopher Santoro. Map and graphics on pages 9 and 39 by Westgraphix LLC.

The photographs in this book are used by permission and through the courtesy of:
Front cover: Dennis Morris/iStockphotos and Lisa J. Goodman/Getty Images (inset).
Alamy: Nadia Mackenzie, 4 (bottom); Visions of America, LLC, 8, 38; Jeff Greenberg, 11; Robert Clay, 12; Cameron Davidson, 13; Tom Till, 14; Gene Ahrens, 16; Harold Smith, 18; Pat & Chuck Blackley, 22; Andre Jenny, 28, 69; Bubbles Photolibrary, 50; Stock Connection Blue, 52, 74; MBI, 49; North Wind Picture Archives, 62; AGStockUSA, 64; National Geographic Image Collection, 70; Vespasian, 73. **AP Images:** Dee Marvin, 48. Corbis: 33; Bettmann, 34. **Delaware Department of Natural Resources and Environmental Control:** 19. **Courtesy of DuPont:** 66, 68. **Getty Images:** 51, 55; Lisa J. Goodman, 4 (top); Altrendo Nature, 5; Willard Clay, 20 (bottom); Gary Meszaros / Visuals Unlimited, Inc., 21; Walker Evans/Time & Life Pictures, 30; William Thomas Cain, 36; Stan Honda/AFP, 39; Hulton Archive, 44, 66; AFP, 45, 57; Randy Wells, 46; Collegiate Images, 49; Cosmo Condina, 63; Jake Rajs, 68; G Fiume, 72. **Library of Congress:** Rep# LC-USZ62-40247, 31. **Courtesy Negro League Baseball Museum, Inc.:** 45. **North Wind Picture Archives:** 24; 26. **Shutterstock:** Dennis Donohue, 20 (top); Mandy Ggodbehar, 60; bsankow, 71. **U.S. Fish and Wildlife Service:** 17.

Printed in Malaysia (T).
135642

CONTENTS

State Flower: Peach Blossom

In the late 1800s, peaches were a booming industry in Delaware. The peach blossom was adopted as the state flower in 1895. However, much of the state's peach industry was soon wiped out by a disease called the peach yellows. Today, the peach blossom remains a symbol of Delaware's proud farming history.

State Insect: Ladybug

In 1974, a second-grade class from a school in Milford led the effort to make the ladybug the state insect. The state legislature approved the idea in April of that year. Five other states have since adopted the ladybug as their official insect.

State Tree: American Holly

The American holly tree has long been a symbol of the Christmas season. The evergreen tree is known for its thick, pointy leaves and bright red berries. American hollies grow as tall as 60 feet (18 meters).

State Beverage: Milk

Milk was adopted as the official state beverage in 1983. Dairy farms have always been important to Delaware's economy. Milk from Delaware's cows is sold throughout Delaware and to other states and is used in products such as cheese, ice cream, and butter.

State Fossil: Belemnite

In 1996, the belemnite was named Delaware's state fossil. Belemnites are sea creatures that are now extinct, which means that they died out long ago. Scientists have discovered that belemnites are related to certain types of modern-day squid. In Delaware, belemnite fossils are most often found along the Chesapeake and Delaware Canal.

State Marine Animal: Horseshoe Crab

Each spring, hundreds of thousands of horseshoe crabs deposit their eggs on the sandy shores of Delaware Bay. Horseshoe crabs are not true crabs—they are more closely related to scorpions or spiders. They may look scary, but horseshoe crabs are not threatening to people. They feed on worms, clams, and other small sea creatures. The horseshoe crab became Delaware's state marine animal in 2002.

★ 1 ★
The First State

With a land area of just 1,982 square miles (5,133 square kilometers), Delaware is the second-smallest state in the U.S. Only Rhode Island is smaller. Delaware has fewer people than forty-four other states. In fact, nearby Philadelphia, Pennsylvania, is one of several U.S. cities that have more people than all of Delaware. But there is one list on which Delaware will always be number one. On December 7, 1787, Delaware become the first of the thirteen original American states to ratify, or approve, the U.S. Constitution. That's why Delaware's nickname is "the First State."

Delaware may be small, but its history is packed with colorful events. There are reminders of America's past all over the state. Delaware is a state of great natural beauty, with countless opportunities for work and for recreation. Proud Delawareans agree with the state slogan: "It's good being first."

The Landscape

Delaware is just 96 miles (155 km) long, and it is very narrow. The state is only 35 miles (56 km) across at its widest point. Delaware has only three counties, the fewest of any state. Roughly two-thirds of the people

Quick Facts

DELAWARE BORDERS

North	Pennsylvania
South	Maryland
East	New Jersey
	Delaware Bay
	Atlantic Ocean
West	Maryland

Wilmington is the largest city in Delaware.

In Their Own Words

One of the things I love about Delaware is that you can be in downtown Wilmington and an hour later you can be in agricultural country. You can cover an awful lot of ground here in just two hours.

—Delaware governor Jack Markell in a 2009 interview

live in the northern county of New Castle. Wilmington, the largest city in Delaware, is in New Castle County. Kent County in central Delaware is home to Dover, the state capital. Kent and the southernmost county of Sussex are more rural and less heavily populated.

Most of Delaware sits on a long peninsula—a stretch of land that is surrounded by water on three sides. This area, called the Delmarva Peninsula, also includes parts of Maryland and Virginia. The peninsula's name is a combination of the names of those three states. The Delaware River, Delaware Bay, and the Atlantic Ocean border the eastern side of the peninsula. Chesapeake Bay lies on its western side.

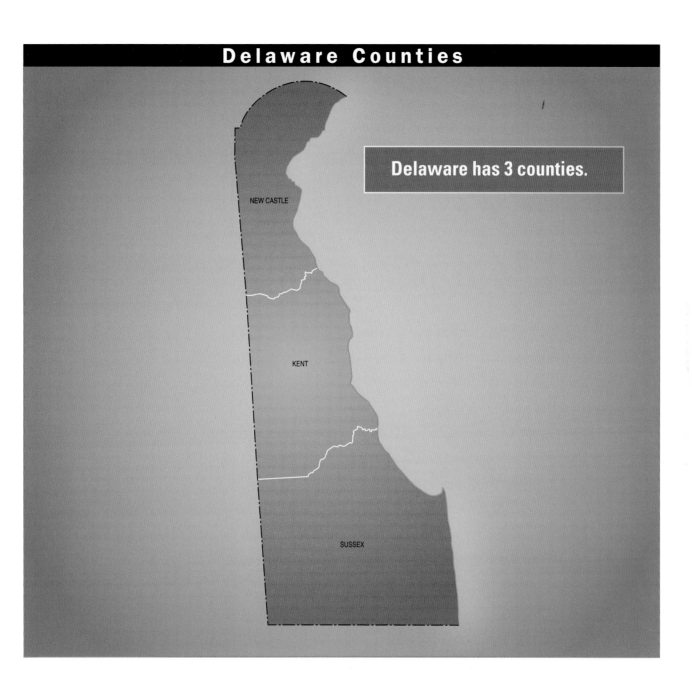

Delaware has 3 counties.

NEW CASTLE

KENT

SUSSEX

Delaware has only two geographic regions. Most of the state is part of the Atlantic Coastal Plain—a narrow belt of lowland that extends from New York to Florida. Delaware is the lowest state in the country. The average elevation is just 60 feet (18 m) above sea level.

A narrow strip of land in northern Delaware is part of a region called the Piedmont. This area of gently rolling hills lies between the Atlantic Coastal Plain and the Appalachian Mountains. Delaware's highest point is found in this area, very close to the Pennsylvania border. A spot near Ebright Road in New Castle County rises 448 feet (137 m) above sea level. Delaware's highest point is actually much lower than the lowest point in many other states.

The marshy land in the southern part of the state forms the famous Great Cypress Swamp. The 30,000-acre (12,140-hectare) swamp is also known as the Great Pocomoke Swamp.

Water Tour

Delaware has 381 miles (613 km) of shoreline—a surprising amount for such a small state. Much of the coast borders Delaware Bay. This area has many shallow coves, sandy beaches, and marshy areas.

Delaware meets the Atlantic Ocean on the eastern edge of Sussex County. The sandy ocean coastline stretches 28 miles (45 km), from the Maryland border in the south to Cape Henlopen at the mouth of Delaware Bay. Rehoboth Beach and Bethany Beach are two of Delaware's most popular tourist destinations. A large part of this coastal area is a low sand bar that separates the ocean from the Rehoboth and Indian River bays.

Many small islands dot the Delaware coastline. The largest are Pea Patch Island and Reedy Island in the Delaware River. Pea Patch Island is home to Fort Delaware State Park. During the Civil War (1861–1865), the fort was used as a prison. Fenwick Island is near the state's southern border. It is a busy vacation spot during the summer.

A low sandy ridge extends north and south through the state just inside Delaware's western border. This ridge is the edge of one of the state's watersheds (land areas draining into bodies of water). The

Quick Facts

UNIQUE BOUNDARY

Delaware's northern border has a unique rounded shape. The border was determined in an equally unique way. A 12-mile (19-km) circular boundary was drawn from the center of the New Castle Court House. That semicircle forms Delaware's border with Pennsylvania.

state's rivers flow either east into the Delaware River or Delaware Bay, or west into Chesapeake Bay. The Delaware River starts in New York State and flows south for more than 300 miles (483 km) before emptying into Delaware Bay. The river is one of the key shipping routes on the East

Delaware's Rehoboth Beach is a popular destination for tourists.

Fort Delaware State Park is located on Pea Patch Island.

Coast. A human-made waterway—the
Chesapeake and Delaware Canal—
cuts across the state just south of
Wilmington. The canal connects
Delaware Bay and Chesapeake Bay.
These waterways played a vital role
in Delaware's economic development
by linking the state with major cities,
especially Philadelphia and Baltimore.

Climate

Delaware has a moderate climate.
Summers in most of the state are
humid, with temperatures averaging
between 70 and 80 degrees Fahrenheit

Quick Facts

HIGHS AND LOWS
The highest recorded
temperature in Delaware's
history occurred in
Millsboro in July 1930.
It was 110 °F (43 °C). The
state's lowest temperature
was also recorded at
Millsboro. On January 17,
1893, the thermometer
dropped to a very chilly
−17 °F (−27 °C).

The leaves on Delaware's trees change color in the cooler fall temperatures.

(21 to 27 degrees Celsius). Ocean breezes make coastal areas a little cooler than the rest of the state. As summer turns to fall, leaves on trees begin to change colors. Residents and visitors alike enjoy the cooler weather and vivid colors of fall.

Winters in the First State are not as harsh as winters in more northern states. The mountainous regions of Pennsylvania block cold northwestern winds from hitting Delaware. The average winter temperature is about 36 °F (2 °C). Warm ocean currents keep coastal areas warmer than inland areas. The amount of snowfall varies from the north to the south. Wilmington gets about 20 inches (51 centimeters) of snow each year. Towns in Sussex County often get far less.

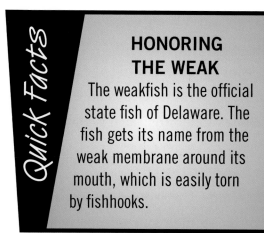

Plant and Animal Life

About 30 percent of Delaware is covered by forests. Delaware and the whole Delmarva Peninsula are in a zone that includes both northern and southern plant life. Trees common to northern states are abundant, including oak, maple, hickory, and poplar. Trees that are found mainly in southern states, such as bald cypress, sweet gum, and loblolly pine, also thrive in Delaware.

From March to October, Delaware's level fields and meadows seem to be carpeted in wildflowers. The display begins in late winter with the first blossoming of crocuses and violets and extends through the asters and mums of late autumn. A number of flowering plants grow throughout spring and summer, including azaleas, morning glories, trumpet vines, and butterfly weeds. Water lilies and floating hearts add color to the many ponds, while pink and white hibiscus dot the marshy areas. Some swampland is almost impassable because of the thickets of wild blueberry and cranberry.

Delaware also has an abundance of wildlife. Its largest wild animal is deer. The state is home to other animals found in eastern states—rabbits, minks, otters, both red and gray foxes, muskrats, and raccoons. Diamondback terrapin live in marshy areas near the coast, and snapping turtles are common in and around swamps. Amphibians such as frogs, toads, and salamanders also live in the damp areas around water or on wet forest floors.

You are never far from water in Delaware—whether it's the ocean, Delaware Bay, the many rivers and streams, or the state's fifty small lakes and ponds.

All this water brings a great variety of birds to the state, which makes bird-watching a favorite pastime.

More than 275 bird species have been identified within Bombay Hook National Wildlife Refuge on the shore of Delaware Bay. This amazing number includes songbirds, such as blue jays, robins, and cardinals. Shorebirds, such as herons and egrets, and a variety of ducks can also be found on its marshy shores. Each spring, the 16,000-acre (6,475-ha) refuge is a stopping point for migrating shorebirds. Up to one million birds feed along the shores of the bay before continuing their journey north. Similarly, the dunes of Fenwick Island State Park are popular for observing black skimmers, osprey, and piping plovers.

Beautiful flowering plants, like these azaleas, grow throughout Delaware in spring and summer.

Up to one million birds feed at Bombay Hook National Wildlife Refuge every year. More than 275 bird species have been identified there.

The salt water of Delaware Bay and the Atlantic Ocean, along with the many sources of fresh water, provide a great variety of fish. Many people enjoy surf-fishing on the Atlantic beaches or taking chartered boats to search for flounder, rockfish, and weakfish. Closer to shore, the coastal waters provide sea trout, shad, and striped bass. Clamming and crabbing are also popular around Delaware Bay. Freshwater fish in rivers and ponds include bluegill, perch, and catfish.

Caring for the Environment

Lawmakers in Delaware have taken steps to preserve the state's environment and natural resources. By the 1970s, the growth of Delaware's cities and suburbs and the increase in factories and motor vehicles were filling the air with a yellowish haze. In the waterways, the harvest of fish and shellfish dropped off so sharply that many commercial fishers were forced out of the trade.

The Delaware state government passed several laws to reverse these trends. Delaware became one of the first states to establish a department of natural resources and environmental control. In 1971, the Coastal Zone Act stopped the building of any industrial plants along the state's coast.

Despite these efforts, the quality of air and water continued to decline. A government study in 1989 showed that 63 percent of Delaware's lakes, rivers, and streams were not safe for fishing or swimming. Eighty percent of the state's people lived in areas where the air did not meet federal standards.

Delawareans and their state officials have worked hard to reduce pollution. Special "action teams" work to clean up the state's waterways. By using these teams, the government is not tackling these problems alone. The state environmental agency has asked citizens to get involved by studying the sources

Delaware provides many options for both saltwater and freshwater fishing.

of pollution and coming up with strategies to reduce pollution in the state's waterways. Government agencies also closely monitor air quality around the state. Strict laws have been passed to correct and regulate a variety of environmental problems.

Delawareans are also concerned about global warming—the slow increase in worldwide temperatures. One effect of global warming is rising sea levels. This could have a big impact on the wildlife, people, homes, and businesses in coastal areas of Delaware. The state is exploring ways to reduce the use of the fossil fuels. Burning fossil fuels, such as coal, creates energy to produce electricity, but it also contributes to global warming. "Clean" energy sources, such as wind and solar power, are better for the environment. Yet, as of 2009, Delaware got less of its energy from clean sources than any other state.

Quick Facts

YOUNG ENVIRONMENTALISTS

The state of Delaware encourages young people to get involved in helping the environment. The Young Environmentalist of the Year awards honor students who have worked to protect, restore, or improve the state's natural wonders. Any Delaware student can participate. To find out more, visit: www.dnrec.delaware.gov/Admin/Pages/YoungEnv.aspx

Diamondback Terrapin

Diamondback terrapins are medium-size turtles common in the marshes near Delaware's long beachfront. They get their name from the shape of the raised plates on their shells. The females are much larger than the males. A female's shell can measure up to 9 inches (23 cm). Diamondback terrapins feed mainly on crabs, mussels, and clams.

Least Tern

Least terns are members of the gull family, but they are smaller and more graceful than seagulls. The terns' small size led to their name—the least of the terns. The terns migrate to Delaware Bay in mid-April to feast on horseshoe crab eggs.

Bald Cypress

Bald cypress trees are common in the swamps of the Southeast, but they are not found farther north than Delaware's Great Cypress Swamp. The cypress is easy to identify by the bald "knees" that grow from its roots and stick out of the water. Bald cypress trees are cone-bearing, but they lose their needles like other deciduous trees.

Beach Plum

In early autumn, you might spot a few beach visitors picking the beach plums that grow in abundance on low bushes in the sand dunes. The bright blossoms of spring turn into a small, tart fruit that can be made into a thick, tasty jam.

Muskrat

Muskrats look very much like small beavers. A muskrat has brown fur, slightly webbed feet, and a broad, flat tail. Muskrats are found throughout Delaware's marshlands and ponds. Some Delawareans consider muskrat to be a tasty meal.

Tiger Swallowtail

Tiger swallowtails are black-and-yellow butterflies that can be found in Delaware's fields and trees from May through August. The tiger swallowtail was declared the state butterfly in 1999. Before they become butterflies, tiger swallowtails move around as green caterpillars with bright eyespots.

From the Beginning

History seems to be everywhere in Delaware. In one small town after another, you can find carefully preserved village greens, old mills with stone grinding wheels, and even some roads still paved with cobblestones. The influence of the state's American Indian history is easy to spot in many places in southern Sussex County. Delawareans are proud of these reminders of the past and they work hard to preserve and protect that heritage.

Under Four Flags

For many years before the first Europeans arrived, the land of modern-day Delaware was home to small bands of American Indians. The largest group was the Lenape, whom European settlers later called the Delaware. The Lenape lived in small villages close to the Delaware River and Delaware Bay. The men hunted and fished, and the women tended crops, prepared meals, and handled most of the child care. A smaller tribe called the Nanticoke lived to the south and east, closer to Chesapeake Bay.

In 1609, British explorer Henry Hudson became the first European to visit the area. He had been hired by the Dutch East India Company to find a route to the Far East. Hudson briefly sailed into Delaware Bay before turning back and heading farther north up the Atlantic coast. He instead explored the river in New York that is now named for him.

A replica of the *Kalmar Nyckel*, a colonial ship, is available for sails and tours

This illustration shows Swedish settlers landing in Delaware in the 1600s.

The name *Delaware* was given to the bay and the river in 1610. English sea captain Samuel Argall named the bodies of water in honor of Sir Thomas West, Lord De la Warr. West was serving as governor of Virginia—the only English colony in North America at the time. The name was later applied to the land on the western side of Delaware Bay and the southern end of the Delaware River.

Residents of the present-day town of Lewes often call their town "the first town in the first state." It was there that a group of Dutch settlers had hoped to start a colony in 1631. That early settlement was named Zwaanendael, which meant "valley of the swans." The settlement lasted less than two years. After a misunderstanding over stolen property, the Lenape destroyed the settlement and killed all the colonists. That massacre would be the only warfare between American Indians and European colonists in Delaware.

In 1638, a group of Swedish settlers built Fort Christina near present-day Wilmington. They named the fort and a nearby river for the eleven-year-old queen of Sweden. The new colony, named New Sweden, also included settlers from Finland. The leader and first governor of the colony was a Dutchman named Peter Minuit. He had been dismissed as the governor of New Netherland (which included present-day New York). The settlers made a permanent contribution to American life by constructing the first log cabins in America. American pioneers would build these simple structures for the next 250 years.

The Dutch knew that the Delaware River and Delaware Bay were important for trade and shipping. They wanted to gain control of the area. In 1651, they built Fort Casimir at the future site of the city of New Castle. The Swedes drove them out in 1654, but the Dutch stormed back and took over the fort and Fort Christina in 1655. Dutch control did not last long, either. In 1664, a powerful English fleet sailed into Delaware Bay and quickly forced the Dutch to surrender.

In 1681, to satisfy a debt, King Charles II of England gave a huge tract of land to William Penn, who established the colony of Pennsylvania. But the new colony did not have any waterways that led to the ocean. To solve that problem, the English gave Penn the land around the Delaware River. The area became known as the Lower Counties of Pennsylvania. The people in the three counties—New Castle, Kent, and Sussex—did not think they had enough say in the Pennsylvania government. In 1704, Penn agreed to let the Lower Counties set up their own assembly.

In Their Own Words

Our people are mostly settled upon the upper rivers, which are pleasant and sweet, and generally bounded with good land.

—William Penn, describing Delaware during his first visit to America in 1683

The town of New Castle became the capital of the Lower Counties. Today, a visual reminder of Delaware's unique history can be seen there. The New Castle Court House displays the flags of all four nations that controlled the area at different times—Sweden, the Netherlands, Great Britain, and the United States.

The Fight for Independence

By the 1770s, many people in the American colonies were calling for freedom from British rule. The colonists were tired of paying taxes to the British while having little say in how they were governed.

William Penn addresses Swedish colonists in New Castle.

They fought for their independence during the American Revolution (1775–1783).

Delaware played an important part in the revolution. In July 1776, the Second Continental Congress met in Philadelphia to vote on the Declaration of Independence. There was no guarantee that the Declaration would be approved. Not all colonists wanted to break free from British rule. The two Delaware delegates in attendance were split. The third delegate, Caesar Rodney, was back in Delaware. When this news reached Rodney, he knew what he had to do. He rode through the night on horseback and arrived in time to break the tie in the Delaware delegation. Delaware voted for independence on July 2, and the Declaration of Independence was approved on July 4.

In a way, Delaware's true declaration of independence had come a few weeks earlier. On June 15, 1776, the assembly had voted to separate from both the Pennsylvania colony and from English rule. The Lower Counties became known as Delaware State.

About four thousand soldiers from Delaware fought during the Revolution. However, only one brief battle was fought in Delaware, in September 1777. The British occupied Wilmington soon after. The Delaware state government moved south from nearby New Castle to Dover for safety. Dover has been Delaware's capital ever since.

Quick Facts

MR. PRESIDENT
In March 1777, Caesar Rodney was elected president—of Delaware! At the time, the leader of the Delaware government was called the president, not the governor.

In Wilmington, a statue honors Caesar Rodney, who played an important part in getting the Declaration of Independence approved.

The colonies won their independence in 1783. A Constitutional Convention was held in Philadelphia in the summer of 1787. The new Constitution had to be ratified, or accepted, by the thirteen states. Each state held a special convention to debate and vote on the Constitution. On December 7, Delaware became the first state to approve it.

The 1800s

For much of its history, Delaware was mainly a farming state. The fast-moving streams and rivers provided waterpower for mills. These mills made Delaware an important center for processing flour and other foods that were sold in nearby cities, especially Philadelphia and Baltimore. In 1802, the du Pont family started a gunpowder mill on the banks of Brandywine Creek near Wilmington. Throughout the 1800s and early 1900s, the DuPont mills produced most of the nation's gunpowder.

Trade and manufacturing gradually became more important to Delaware. The state's mills produced not only flour and gunpowder but also a variety of products, including cloth and paper. The city of Wilmington became a center for both manufacturing and trade. The methods for transporting goods in and out of Delaware improved. In 1829, the Chesapeake and Delaware Canal was opened. The canal reduced the water route from Philadelphia to Baltimore by nearly 300 miles (485 km). From the late 1830s on, railroads steadily grew in importance and water transportation declined.

In the 1860s, tensions between the North and the South led to the Civil War (1861–1865). Eleven southern states broke away from the rest of the country

This building was part of the original du Pont family gunpowder mill. It was built along Brandywine Creek, north of Wilmington.

FAMOUS CONDUCTOR

Thomas Garrett was Delaware's most famous "conductor" on the Underground Railroad. His friend Harriet Tubman often brought runaway slaves to his home. In 1848, Garrett was arrested and fined for helping slaves, but he refused to give up his fight against slavery. Before the Civil War ended, he helped more than 2,700 slaves escape to freedom.

and formed the Confederate States of America. One of the main reasons for the war was slavery. The first slaves brought to the British North American colonies that became the United States had been kidnapped from Africa in the 1600s. By the mid–1800s, Southern farmers relied on slaves as field workers. But most states in the North did not allow slavery.

Delaware struggled with the issue of slavery. In 1860, about 20,000 free African Americans lived in the state. Many white Delawareans wanted to see slavery abolished, or ended. Some helped slaves on the Underground Railroad—a secret network of people who helped slaves escape to freedom in the years before the Civil War. Some Delaware homes and meeting houses served as "stations," or safe hiding places, for slaves on their journey north.

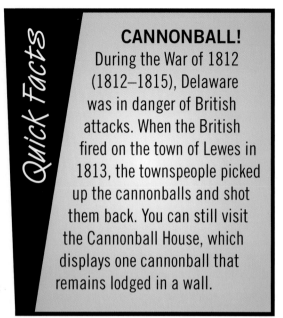
However, Delawareans still owned about 1,800 slaves. Though Delaware stayed in the Union when the Civil War began, several hundred of its people fought for the Confederacy. After nearly four years of bloody battles, the Confederacy surrendered in the spring of 1865, and the country was unified once again. The Thirteenth Amendment to the U.S. Constitution officially abolished slavery nationwide in December 1865. Yet many decades would pass before African Americans in Delaware, and other states, would truly have equal rights.

The Twentieth Century

In the twentieth century, industry changed in many ways—and the lives of Delawareans changed with it. The use of new sources of power, including steam and electricity, led to new industries in the Wilmington area. In addition to gunpowder, factories made ships, railroad cars, and machinery. These industries were important for America during World War I (in which the United States fought from 1917 to 1918) and World War II (in which the United States fought from 1941 to 1945).

DuPont supplied much of the gunpowder used by Americans and their allies. Shipyards built war vessels. The increased production in factories and shipyards provided jobs for many Delawareans. While many men fought overseas, women in the United States served their country by working in

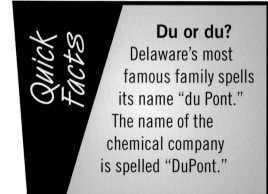

Delaware has always been a farming state. In this photo, farmers were bringing watermelons to load onto railroad cars.

factories and other industries that helped the war effort. Many Delawarean women worked at jobs that were available only to men before the war.

Delaware has continued to change since World War II. DuPont moved toward producing chemicals for paints and other household products. Most of the "heavy" industries have been replaced by "light" industries, which make such products as processed foods, medical instruments, and electronic components. Today, Delawareans try to continue to adapt to changing times.

Women helped the war effort in World War II by serving in the military. These women worked as pilots at the New Castle Army Air Base near Wilmington.

★ **1609** Henry Hudson sails into Delaware Bay and claims the entire area for the Dutch.

★ **1631** Dutch colonists set up the first European settlement in Delaware.

★ **1638** Swedish colonists establish Fort Christina at modern-day Wilmington.

★ **1655** The Dutch again take control of what is now Delaware.

★ **1664** The British take control from the Dutch of present-day Delaware.

★ **1682** William Penn founds the Pennsylvania colony, which includes the three Lower Counties (modern-day Delaware).

★ **1704** William Penn allows the Lower Counties to have their own government.

★ **1776** Delaware separates from Pennsylvania. Caesar Rodney rides to Philadelphia to cast Delaware's deciding vote for the Declaration of Independence.

★ **1787** On December 7, Delaware becomes the first state to ratify the new U.S. Constitution.

★ **1802** The du Pont family establishes a gunpowder mill along Brandywine Creek, north of Wilmington.

★ **1829** The Chesapeake and Delaware Canal opens.

★ **1838** Railroads connect Philadelphia and Baltimore, encouraging industrial development in northern Delaware.

★ **1917–1918** U.S. participation in World War I stimulates Delaware's industries.

★ **1941–1945** U.S. participation in World War II expands Delaware's industries.

★ **1981** Changes in state laws draw out-of-state banks to establish offices in Delaware. Many more banks and other business follow in the coming decades.

★ **2000** Delawareans elect their first female governor, Ruth Ann Minner.

★ **2008** Delaware senator Joe Biden is elected vice president of the United States. He and President Barack Obama are sworn in on January 20, 2009.

The People

There are only five states with fewer people than Delaware. Those states are North Dakota, South Dakota, Alaska, Vermont, and Wyoming. But because of its small size, Delaware has a high population density, or number of people per square mile. The population density, in fact, is among the highest in the country. In 2007, Delaware had 448 people per square mile. The national average is about 85 people per square mile. The state is far from crowded, however. Delaware's biggest city, Wilmington, has only about 72,000 people.

Delaware has seen a remarkable mixing of people and cultures since the first Europeans arrived in the early 1600s. The original residents—the American Indians—witnessed the arrival of settlers from the Netherlands, Sweden, and Finland, followed by England in the 1660s. In addition, small numbers of slaves were brought from Africa and sold to colonists.

According to 2007 U.S. Census Bureau estimates, nearly 75 percent of Delawareans are white. About 20 percent are black. More than half the population in Wilmington is African American. Asians account for 3 percent of the state population. Most of these people have roots in India, China, or the Philippines. American Indians represent less than 1 percent. People who consider themselves Hispanic or Latino make up more than 6 percent of the state's population. Most of these people are of Mexican or Puerto Rican descent.

Delaware is a small state, but it has a diverse population.

A family celebrates at the Puerto Rican Festival in Wilmington.

Two or More Races
16,978 (2.0%)

Some Other Race
18,623 (2.1%)

Asian
25,372 (3.0%)

Black or African American
175,682 (20.3%)

Native Hawaiian and Other Pacific Islander
532 (0.0%)*

American Indian and Alaska Native
2,223 (0.0%)*

White
625,354 (72.3%)

Total Population
864,764

Hispanics or Latinos:
- 56,153 people
- 6.5% of the state's population

Hispanics or Latinos may be of any race.

Note: The pie chart shows the racial breakdown of the state's population based on the categories used by the U.S. Bureau of the Census. The Census Bureau reports information for Hispanics or Latinos separately, since they may be of any race. Percentages in the pie chart may not add to 100 because of rounding.

* Less than 0.1%.

Source: U.S. Bureau of the Census, 2007 American Community Survey

American Indians

The makeup of Delaware's population changed a great deal during the 1700s. One change was the sharp decline in the American Indian population. Many Lenape (later known as the Delaware) died from diseases brought by Europeans, such as smallpox. Much of the American Indians' land was taken over by European settlers. Most of the Indians in Delaware moved west, joining other Indian groups beyond the Appalachian Mountains. By 1750, only a few thousand American Indians remained in Delaware. The Nanticokes, the only remaining group of the Delaware, live in central Delaware and number about five hundred people.

Today, Delaware's American Indians keep their traditions—while also enjoying modern activities.

LENAPE STRAW GAME

**The Lenape originated this game using colored reeds.
It is a game of skill and chance, similar to pick-up sticks.**

WHAT YOU NEED

15 straws or long lollipop sticks
(found in craft stores)

Black or red paint or markers

A small paintbrush

A crochet hook or a sharp pencil

Paint or color the straws with these patterns:

One with stripes

One with a solid color on one end and stripes on the other end

Two with dots

Two with dots at each end, leaving the center blank

Two with stripes at each end, leaving the center blank

Two with a solid color at one end, leaving the other end blank

Two with stripes on one end and dots on the other end

Leave three straws blank.

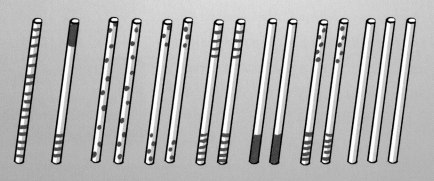

Once your straws are dry, begin playing the game. To play, the first player gathers the straws and tosses them onto a blanket or rug.

With the help of the crochet hook or pencil, the player tries to lift a single straw without moving any other straws. (The Lenape used a bent quill to help them lift the straws.) A player earns points for each straw that is successfully lifted.

Point system:

Straw with stripes: 75 points

Straw half solid and half striped: 50 points

Each of the two straws with polka dots: 25 points

Each of the two straws with dots at each end: 20 points

Each of the two straws with stripes at each end: 15 points

Each of the two straws solid at one end, other end blank: 0 points

Each of the two straws striped at one end, dots at other end: 5 points

Each of the three blank straws: 1 point

A player's turn ends when he or she moves a straw other than the targeted straw. The player adds up the points earned.

The next player gathers all straws and proceeds in the same manner. The first player to reach 100 points wins.

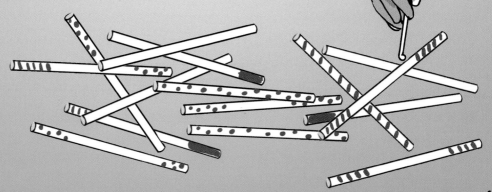

Immigrants from Europe

As the American Indian population declined, the white population increased. The 1700s brought newcomers called the Scots-Irish; these people came from the area that today is known as Northern Ireland. In the 1800s, troubles in Europe brought two new groups. Starting in the 1820s, large numbers of immigrants came from Ireland, seeking to escape poverty. Immigration from Ireland increased further in the 1840s, when disease destroyed the potato crop—the main source of food for most poor families in Ireland. Large numbers of German immigrants arrived in the 1840s and 1850s, driven from their homeland by political unrest. Like many immigrants, both groups faced prejudice from many native-born Americans. By about 1900, however, both groups had melted into the mainstream of American life.

In the late 1800s, the development of industry, especially in and around Wilmington, drew a new wave of immigrants from Southern and Eastern Europe. Poles, Slavs, Jews, Italians, and other groups arrived. They found work in factories and on the railroads.

A Mixing of Religions

The first European settlers represented different Protestant religions. The Dutch belonged to the Dutch Reform Church, and the Swedes were mostly Lutheran. Many English settlers were members of another Protestant group, the Episcopal Church. Small groups of Quakers also came to Delaware from Pennsylvania. Pennsylvania's founder, William Penn, was a Quaker. The Quakers were members of the Religious Society of Friends. Although few in number, the Quakers had a strong influence in Delaware. They strongly opposed slavery—in Delaware and in the rest of the United States.

The 1700s and 1800s saw the arrival of large numbers of Presbyterians and Roman Catholics. In the late 1700s, traveling preachers helped spread the beliefs of Methodism. The Methodist Episcopal Church soon became the largest in Delaware. Today, Roman Catholics and Methodists are the two biggest religious groups in the state.

GOING TO CHAPEL

Barrat's Chapel, near Frederica, Delaware, is the oldest Methodist building in the United States. There, in 1784, two preachers decided to organize the Methodist Episcopal Church. Today, the chapel is known as "the cradle of American Methodism."

John Dickinson: Founding Father

John Dickinson is called "the Penman of the Revolution." He was born in 1732. In his writings, he argued that the colonies should unite and demand more rights from Great Britain. However, Dickinson did not want the colonies to break free from Britain. Once independence was declared, though, he drafted the Articles of the Confederation—the first constitution of the United States. Later, he represented Delaware at the Constitutional Convention in 1787 and used his influence to help get the U.S. Constitution ratified.

Thomas Macdonough: Naval Officer

Born in what is now Macdonough, Delaware, in 1783, Thomas Macdonough gained fame in the wars against the Barbary Pirates of North Africa from 1805 to 1807. During the War of 1812 between the United States and Great Britain, Macdonough was placed in command of a small fleet on Lake Champlain. His orders were to hold off a British invasion fleet coming south from Canada. Macdonough captured the British fleet and saved New York and Vermont from invasion.

Howard Pyle: Artist

Howard Pyle was born in Wilmington in 1853. Pyle studied art, and in 1876, he had his first illustration published (illustrating a poem). Pyle continued to create beautiful illustrations for magazines and books and also worked on murals and other paintings. His work won praise for its historical accuracy and detail. Pyle later became a teacher and offered art lessons for free.

Annie Jump Cannon: Astronomer

Annie Jump Cannon was born in Dover in 1863. She later became an astronomer at the Harvard Observatory, where she gained fame for developing a system for classifying stars. She published her results in a huge, nine-volume catalog. Her system is still used throughout the world and helped to make astronomy a more important branch of science.

William Julius "Judy" Johnson: Baseball Player

Born in 1900, Judy Johnson was a terrific baseball player who never got a chance to compete in the major leagues. Before 1947, African Americans were allowed to play only in the Negro Leagues. Johnson was a great hitter and an excellent fielder at third base. The Wilmington native was elected to the Baseball Hall of Fame in 1975.

Joe Biden: Politician

Born in Scranton, Pennsylvania, in 1942, Joe Biden moved with his family to Claymont, Delaware, in 1953. He later attended the University of Delaware—as did his wife, Jill. In 1972, Biden was elected to the U.S. Senate. The popular senator was reelected six times. In 2008, Barack Obama ran for president and selected Biden as his running mate. On November 4, Biden was elected the forty-seventh vice president of the United States.

Delaware After 1900

America's involvement in World War I and World War II led to a sharp increase in city populations, especially in Wilmington. Large numbers of people, including many African Americans from the South, came to work in the factories and shipyards.

After World War II, many people left Wilmington for its suburbs. Many newcomers to the state also moved to the suburbs. Today, about half of Delaware's people live within commuting distance of Wilmington.

A small community of Amish people settled in Delaware, near Dover.

Delaware experienced its largest population growth from 1950 to 1960. The continued development of the state's chemical industry drew scientists, technicians, and other workers from other parts of the United States and from other countries.

Most of southern Delaware remains rural. The area's population is as diverse as the rest of the state's. Kent County, for example, is home to prosperous dairy and potato farms operated by Polish-American families who moved from Long Island, New York. At Iron Hill, there is a large group of people from Finland who came after World War I. A small Amish settlement lies near Dover. The Amish people are a Christian sect. They live simply on farms and do not rely on modern machinery.

Working Together for Education

For many years, education was not unified throughout the state. While the early colonists valued education, most schools were operated by local churches, and the quality of the education was uneven. In about 1700, wealthy English families began sending their sons to schools in England. They educated their daughters at home or at boarding schools in Philadelphia.

Delaware established a fund for schools in 1796, but the money was not put to use for years. In 1829, a new law set up the state's first true public school system. Still, the quality of education in many schools was poor. Conditions were even worse for African-American students, who were not allowed to attend the same schools as white children. In the 1920s, a member of the du Pont family donated a large sum of his own money to improve the schools. Much of the money went to build new schools for African Americans.

In 1954, the U.S. Supreme Court ruled that schools could no longer be segregated. All schools must be open to black students as well as white students. However, schools in some Delaware cities, especially Wilmington, did not want to change. In 1978, the city started a court-ordered program to integrate the schools. Black students from Wilmington were bused to schools in the suburbs. White students from the suburbs were bused to schools in the city.

The state continues to face educational challenges. For years, the average national test scores of white students have been much higher than those of black students. But the results from 2009 showed that African-American students in Delaware are closing the gap faster than students in most states. That was a positive sign for the future of education in the First State.

Delaware has made progress in improving its schools. Here, former first lady Laura Bush reads to a group of students.

Members of the University of Delaware Blue Hens marching band play during a game at Tubby Raymond Field/Delaware Stadium in Newark, Delaware.

Higher Learning

Delaware is home to two well-known public universities. Founded in 1743, the University of Delaware is the oldest college in the state. About 20,000 students are enrolled at the school. Delaware State University is a historically black college that was founded in 1891.

★ The Delaware Kite Festival

On the Friday before Easter, hundreds of kites of every size and shape soar above Cape Henlopen State Park in Lewes during the Delaware Kite Festival.

★ Old Dover Day

Held on the first Saturday in May, Old Dover Day celebrates the city's rich heritage. Residents and visitors can tour stately old homes (including the birthplace of Annie Jump Cannon), the State House, Legislative Hall, and, just south of town, the John Dickinson Plantation.

★ Wilmington Garden Day

During Wilmington Garden Day, held in May each year, visitors can explore some of the most famous and elegant gardens in the country, including those at the Winterthur Museum and the Nemours Mansion.

★ Separation Day

The people of Delaware celebrate their "first" independence day each June 15. On that day in 1776, the Delaware assembly voted to break free from the Pennsylvania colony and from Great Britain.

★ Delaware State Fair

July is the month for the Delaware State Fair at Harrington. The fair offers traditional displays, such as farm produce and cattle, as well as a gigantic fireworks show.

★ Nanticoke Indian Powwow

This colorful event, held each September in Millsboro, includes traditional Nanticoke clothing, crafts, and foods.

★ Brandywine Arts Festival

In September, the Brandywine Arts Festival draws artists and art lovers to an area noted for the paintings and illustrations of artist Howard Pyle.

★ Punkin Chunkin World Championship

This pumpkin-throwing contest is held the first weekend after Halloween in Sussex County. Contestants create special machines to launch pumpkins thousands of feet.

How the Government Works

The constitution of a state is its framework of government. Much like the U.S. Constitution, it describes the duties of the state government's three branches: the executive, the legislative, and the judicial. The executive branch, headed by the governor, runs the affairs of the state. The legislature makes laws. The judicial branch is the system of courts that settles disputes or hears cases when laws are broken.

During America's colonial period, the legislature in each colony could make its own laws, but the British monarch (the king or queen) could reject any law that he or she did not like. In 1776, when the Continental Congress approved the Declaration of Independence, the Thirteen Colonies became thirteen independent states and could write their own state constitutions. Delaware had a constitution ready by the end of 1776.

Over the next hundred-plus years, the legislature wrote three new constitutions. The state constitution in use today was written in 1897. But Delawareans have added amendments, or made changes, to the constitution more than a hundred times. The process for amending the Delaware constitution is different from the process in any other state. The change must be approved by two-thirds of the legislature. Then the proposed amendment is posted in newspapers in each county before the next election. The legislature votes again. If the proposal again wins two-thirds of the vote, the amendment is officially

Delaware's lawmakers meet
in Legislative Hall in Dover.

EXECUTIVE ★ ★ ★ ★ ★ ★ ★ ★

The governor is the head of the state. He or she is responsible for approving or rejecting laws passed by the legislative branch. The governor prepares the state budget and suggests new laws. Along with the lieutenant governor, the attorney general, and the treasurer, the governor is elected to a four-year term. The governor is allowed to serve only two terms.

LEGISLATIVE ★ ★ ★ ★ ★ ★ ★ ★

The general assembly makes state laws. It is divided into two parts. The twenty-one senators are elected for four-year terms. The forty-one members of the house of representatives serve two-year terms. There is no limit on the number of terms a member of the general assembly can serve.

JUDICIAL ★ ★ ★ ★ ★ ★ ★ ★

All judges are appointed by the governor with the approval of the senate. These judges serve twelve-year terms. The highest court, the state supreme court, hears appeals from lower courts and can decide whether a law violates some part of the state constitution. Below the supreme court is the superior court, for criminal and civil cases. The court of chancery hears cases involving business disputes. The lowest courts hear cases involving matters such as family disputes or traffic offenses.

added to the constitution. The governor cannot veto, or reject, a constitutional amendment.

How a Bill Becomes a Law

As in other states, before a law is passed in Delaware, it must go through an established process. Most laws begin with a suggestion or an idea from a Delaware resident or a member of the state legislature. The proposed law is called a bill.

The Delaware state legislature is called the general assembly. Like the U.S. Congress, it has a senate and a house of representatives. A bill may be introduced in either the senate or the house. From there, it is assigned to a committee. The committee members examine the bill, hold hearings, or meetings, and may revise the bill. The committee can reject the bill and decide not to present it to the entire house. But if the committee is satisfied with the bill, it is presented to the rest of the house.

The bill is read to the house three times. After the second reading, legislators can revise or amend the bill. They usually debate the bill after the third reading. After the third reading and the debates, the legislators vote on the bill.

FAMOUS FIRSTS
In 1984, S. B. Woo was elected lieutenant governor of Delaware. The lieutenant governor is like the vice president of the state. At the time, Woo was the highest-ranking Chinese American elected to public office. He served one term. In 1992, Ruth Ann Minner became the state's first female lieutenant governor. Later, she became Delaware's first female governor and served two terms.

Ruth Ann Minner, shown here in 2005 at a ceremonial bill signing, became Delaware's first female lieutenant governor in 1992.

If the bill is approved, it is sent to the other house. There, it goes through a very similar process.

If both houses agree on the bill, it is then sent to the governor. If the governor approves the bill, he or she can sign it into law. The governor may also make changes to the bill and send it back to the general assembly. If the governor does not take any action, the bill will automatically become law after a certain amount of time. The governor can also veto the bill. The vetoed bill can still become law if two-thirds of the members of both houses vote to override the governor's veto.

Local Government

The counties—New Castle, Kent, and Sussex—are the primary units for local government. New Castle and Sussex governments consist of an elected council and council president. Kent County uses an older system. It has an elected board of commissioners called the "levy court." The name comes from the old tradition of levying, or collecting, taxes.

In addition, Delaware's large towns and cities generally elect a mayor and a council. A few hire a city manager rather than a mayor. Near the state's northern border, three villages known as the Ardens do not have any official government. Citizens work together to solve problems in the villages. The Ardens operate according to the ideas of Henry George, an author in the late 1800s. The townspeople own the land together rather than individually.

National Level

Like all states, Delaware is represented in the U.S. Congress in Washington, D.C. Each state elects two U.S. senators. Senators serve six-year terms,

Quick Facts

ALL IN THE FAMILY
Joe Biden's oldest son, Joe III (called Beau), is also involved in Delaware politics. In 2006, Beau was elected state attorney general—the top law officer in the state. Beau is a member of the Delaware National Guard. He served in Iraq from 2008 to 2009 and kept his post as attorney general.

Joe Biden and his son Beau acknowledge the crowd during the 2008 Democratic National Convention. Joe Biden was sworn in as vice president of the United States in January 2009.

and they can be elected as many times as voters choose. Delaware's longest-serving U.S. senator was Joe Biden. He was first elected in 1972 at the age of 29. He served until January 2009, when he gave up his position to become vice president of the United States.

Delawareans elect one person to the U.S. House of Representatives. A state's population determines its number of representatives. In 2010, Delaware was one of seven states that have only one representative. California has the most people and the most representatives of any state (53 in 2010).

Citizen Leadership

The people of Delaware have a history of using their own money to fund important state projects. In the 1820s, for instance, Delawareans knew that a

Contacting Lawmakers

★ ★ ★ ★ ★ ★ ★ ★ ★ ★ ★ ★ ★

The contact information for Delaware's governor, members of the general assembly, and representatives in the U.S. Congress is available online. For names, phone numbers, and e-mail addresses, visit

www.delaware.gov/egov/portal.nsf/ portal/elected

canal to connect the Delaware River and Chesapeake Bay would be good for business. The canal would make transporting products cheaper and faster. They had seen how the recently completed Erie Canal across New York State had reduced the cost of shipping farm products by 90 percent. But Delaware's general assembly had recently established a fund for schools, and there was not enough money left for a canal.

Business owners from Delaware, Pennsylvania, and Maryland decided to build the canal on their own. They raised money, formed a company, and built the Chesapeake and Delaware Canal. The 14-mile (22.5-km) canal was completed in 1829. With locks to raise and lower ships, the canal greatly cut the time needed to ship products from Philadelphia to Baltimore. In 1919, the federal government bought the canal and deepened it for ocean steamships.

A similar event took place in the early 1900s. The development of the automobile created the need for paved roads, especially running north-south. The farms and towns of southern Delaware were not connected to cities in the northern part of the state. But there was no money in the state budget to build the needed roadway. T. Coleman du Pont, a member of the state's famous business family, undertook the task with his own money in 1911. The DuPont Highway was completed in 1924. Du Pont then turned it over to the highway department as a family gift to the state.

These are bold examples of how residents can work together to improve their state. Delawareans do not have to be wealthy to make a difference, however. In 2009, a Wilmington high school student won a national award for her community service. She volunteered with Success Won't Wait, a program that gives books to disadvantaged students and adults. The program was started by a Delaware college student in 2002. To date, Success Won't Wait has collected more than 100,000 books. People can also get involved by calling, writing, and e-mailing their representatives in the state government in Dover. They can suggest new laws, discuss problems in their community, and work together to make Delaware a better place to live.

The Success Won't Wait program gives books to many students.

Making a Living

The morning mists rose above the streams and rivers of northern Delaware. As the sun glistened on the lapping water of mill wheels, the steady power of the water turned large stone grinding wheels. This quiet scene was repeated every day through the early 1800s. Farm wagons would drive up to the stone millhouses with loads of corn or wheat to be ground into meal or flour. Mills were also used for cutting lumber and for making paper and textiles. One of the early mills, established on the Brandywine Creek in 1802, was used to manufacture gunpowder.

The early settlers built their farms and plantations close to the rivers and streams to make use of the waterways for transportation. There were few roads in Delaware until the 1900s, so transportation by horse-drawn vehicles was slow. Boats or sailing ships were more convenient.

In the colonial years, many of Delaware's farms and plantations grew tobacco. Ships picked up the product from the docks and transported it to markets in Europe. Tobacco rapidly wore out the soil, however, and Delawareans searched for new sources of farm income. Many in the northern part of the state turned to wheat. Corn became the major crop in southern Delaware.

In the 1800s, the growing and selling of peaches created a great wave of prosperity for the state's farmers. The crops were shipped by the waterways. After 1840, they were sent by railroad to city markets, especially in Philadelphia

Delawareans no longer have to travel by horseback, but riding horses is still a popular hobby.

and New York. Peach tree orchards in the state included more than 800,000 trees. But the peach boom did not last. The peaches were stricken by a blight, or disease, called the yellows, and the orchards declined steadily after 1900. Peach growing picked up after World War II. Today, Delaware growers produce about 2 million pounds (907,100 kilograms) of peaches each year.

Still Farming

The development of industry, beginning in the late 1800s, became a larger source of income, but farming has remained very important. As the peach orchards declined, many farmers turned to growing other fruits and vegetables. Crops such as beans, peas, tomatoes, berries, and melons were shipped by water or rail. Today these farms are called "truck farms," since road transportation has replaced railroads and ships to move the farm products to market. Many truck farms are operated by part-time farmers.

There are still many farms and pastures along the Delaware River, like this one in Tinicum.

RECIPE FOR PEACH KUCHEN

In 2009, peach pie was named the state dessert of Delaware. Kuchen is like a pie without a top crust.

WHAT YOU NEED

For the crust:

1 stick unsalted butter

$^1/_4$ cup (50 grams) sugar

$1^1/_2$ cup (180 g) all-purpose flour

$^1/_2$ teaspoon (3 g) salt

1 teaspoon (5 milliliters) vanilla

1 teaspoon (4 g) baking powder

1 egg

To make the filling:

5 peaches

$^1/_2$ cup (100 g) sugar

1 tablespoon (15 g) cinnamon

Ask an adult to help you preheat the oven to 350 °F (175 °C). While the oven is heating, mix the butter and sugar for the crust. Add the rest of the crust ingredients and mix. The dough should be crumbly, but it should still hold together. Spread butter or margarine on the sides and bottom of a 9-inch (23-cm) pan. Press the dough into the pan and up against the sides.

Peel, remove the pits from, and cut the peaches into slices. Lay the peach slices on the dough. Sprinkle the peaches with cinnamon and sugar. Bake at 350 °F (175 °C) for 25 to 35 minutes, until the crust is a golden brown.

Have an adult help you remove the kuchen from the oven—it will be hot. When it is cooled, add a little ice cream or whipped cream and enjoy.

This illustration shows an old-fashioned soybean field in Sussex County. Today, soybeans are one of Delaware's most important crops.

Chicken broilers are Delaware's biggest farm product. Delaware farmers raise more than 250 million chickens for their meat. Yet this important industry started by accident. In the early 1920s, Cecile and Wilmer Steele of Ocean View ordered 50 chickens. They wanted to raise the chickens and sell their eggs. But when the Steeles received 500 chickens by mistake, they decided to raise them for their meat. Delaware's broiler industry was born.

Today, Delaware's farm industry continues to thrive. The state is home to about 2,500 farms that cover 500,000 acres (200,000 ha). Sussex County is one of the wealthiest agricultural counties in the country. In addition to corn and wheat, soybeans have become a major crop. Farm families in the extreme south also make holly wreaths during the Christmas season. Dairy and cattle farms are also key parts of the farming economy.

Commercial fishing remains profitable, although pollution problems have reduced the number of fishing boats. Fishing boats and chartered boats are used to catch saltwater fish in Delaware Bay and the ocean. Shellfish harvesting along the coast is profitable as well.

Workers & Industries

Industry	Number of People Working in That Industry	Percentage of All Workers Who Are Working in That Industry
Education and health care	88,658	21.3%
Wholesale and retail businesses	59,876	14.4%
Banking and finance, insurance, and real estate	44,067	10.6%
Manufacturing	42,455	10.2%
Publishing, media, entertainment, hotels, and restaurants	41,820	10.1%
Professionals, scientists, and managers	40,715	9.8%
Construction	36,053	8.7%
Transportation and public utilities	21,087	5.1%
Government	19,733	4.7%
Other services	17,604	4.2%
Farming, fishing, forestry, and mining	3,743	0.9%
Totals	**2,424,534**	**100%**

Notes: Figures above do not include people in the armed forces. "Professionals" includes people such as doctors and lawyers. Percentages may not add to 100 because of rounding.

Source: U.S. Bureau of the Census, 2007 estimates

The DuPont Story

One of the most important people in Delaware's history was an immigrant from Paris, France. Eleuthère Irénée du Pont de Nemours arrived in the United States in 1799. Three years later, he persuaded his father to finance the building of a mill to manufacture gunpowder. The high quality of the product made the company a great success. It rapidly became the country's largest supplier of gunpowder and one of the largest in the world. Since the early 1800s, DuPont has been a mainstay of Delaware's economy. The family no longer owns the company. But family members in each generation have been major figures in state culture and politics.

Wallace Carothers, a chemist, worked for DuPont in the 1920s. His work helped develop nylon, which was used to make parachutes and women's stockings.

MORE FROM DUPONT

Nylon is not the only useful synthetic material developed by DuPont. Kevlar is a super-strong fiber that is used in the bulletproof vests worn by police officers and soldiers. Teflon is a slippery, nonstick substance that is applied to cookware and other products.

In 1912, the federal government ruled that the DuPont Company was a monopoly in the manufacture of gunpowder. A monopoly is a company that controls so much of an industry that it has no competition. As a result, DuPont was divided into three corporations: Atlas, Hercules, and DuPont.

Over the next few years, DuPont moved away from gunpowder production. The company began to focus on the development of chemical products, such as paint and dyes. In the mid–1930s, Wallace Carothers and other DuPont chemists developed nylon. This was a major breakthrough for the company. Nylon was used as a fabric to make parachutes and other products. Its most popular use was in women's stockings.

The DuPont laboratories and a manufacturing plant helped make Wilmington an important industrial center. The city has been called the "chemical capital of the world." The city's location is also ideal for business. Waterways, railroads, and highways place northern Delaware within easy reach of Philadelphia, Washington, DC, and other cities.

Manufacturing

There is much more to industry in Delaware than chemicals, of course. Food processing is a big part of the state's economy. Large plants in Dover, for example, make gelatin, puddings, and other dessert products. Other plants in northern Delaware make baked goods, fish products, and soft drinks. Poultry processing is also an important industry. The completion of the Delaware Memorial Bridge in 1951 linked Delaware with New Jersey. Major automobile companies soon set up assembly plants in Delaware.

Chemical Research

In the late 1930s, the invention of nylon by DuPont scientists caused a sensation worldwide. Nylon is a durable substance that can be spun as fine as silk. It even replaced silk in the manufacture of parachutes during World War II. This breakthrough in the development of synthetic, or human-made, materials led dozens of chemical companies to establish research laboratories in Delaware.

Chickens

Raising chickens has become the largest source of agricultural income in the state. More than eight hundred Delaware farms raise chickens. Much of the corn and soybeans grown in Delaware is used as chicken feed.

Ocean Beaches

Rehoboth Beach and Bethany Beach are the most popular ocean resorts in the state. Both beaches are an easy drive from Pennsylvania, Maryland, New Jersey, and Washington, D.C. In fact, Rehoboth Beach is sometimes called the Nation's Summer Capital because so many people from Washington, D.C., take vacations there. The coast of Delaware Bay is home to other, smaller beaches that locals enjoy.

Truck Farms

Delaware's bridges and roads have given farm families easy access to city markets. Truck farms in Kent and Sussex counties grow table vegetables, such as lettuce, tomatoes, broccoli, beans, peas, and squash. Berries and melons are among the many fruits grown on truck farms.

Museums

Delaware is home to many wonderful museums. The Winterthur Museum near Wilmington has about two hundred rooms devoted to the decorative arts. Its antique furniture, other room decorations, architectural elements, ceramics, and metalwork all date before 1840. The Hagley Museum on Brandywine Creek is located on the site of the original DuPont gunpowder mill. In addition, entire sections of some towns, such as the Old Court House area of New Castle, are "living museums" of buildings from the 1700s and 1800s.

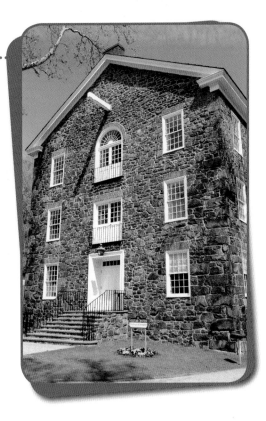

Hogs

Many farms across the state raise hogs. Hog farms sell their livestock to companies all over the state and throughout the country. Some of the livestock is sent to meat processing plants in Delaware. The hogs are used for ham, bacon, and other pork products.

The Delaware Memorial Bridge connects Delaware to New Jersey. Today, more than 80,000 vehicles cross the Delaware River every day.

Government and Tourism

Government is also a major source of employment. Many people have jobs in state and local government offices, in public school systems, and at the U.S. military's Dover Air Force Base.

For a small state, Delaware has a great deal to offer tourists. Visitors enjoy the state's beaches and the clear waters of the bay, rivers, lakes, and streams. The parks and forests are excellent for hiking, mountain biking, camping, and bird-watching. Others come to the state to see the historic sites that honor Delaware's—and the nation's—history.

One of the state's top attractions is Dover Downs. The complex includes a hotel, a casino, and a harness racing track. It is also home to Dover International Speedway. Each year, more than 135,000 fans pack the speedway to watch the top NASCAR drivers in action.

Festivals, fairs, and other events also draw people to Delaware. The state has a number of museums and galleries where people can admire art and other unique treasures. Visitors also love shopping in Delaware's outlets and other retail shops. The state is one of the few that has no sales tax.

Tourism in Delaware brings in money for the state and provides jobs for state residents. The steady growth of tourism creates a wide variety of jobs in service industries, including restaurants, hotels, and motels.

NASCAR fans come to Delaware to watch races at the Dover International Speedway.

THE BLUE ROCKS

Delaware does not have any major sports teams, but it does have the Blue Rocks. The Blue Rocks are a minor league baseball team in Wilmington. Many future Major League stars played for the team, including Carlos Beltran, Johnny Damon, and Jacoby Ellsbury (below).

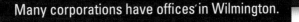

Many corporations have offices in Wilmington.

"The Home of Corporations"

During the 1970s, many Delawareans were out of work. Business and government leaders came up with an unusual solution. Lawmakers changed the state's business laws to attract out-of-state companies, especially banks and credit card companies. Dozens of corporations took advantage of the laws and set up corporate offices in the Wilmington area. Delaware got a new nickname— "the Home of Corporations." These companies created new jobs and brought extra tax income to the state. At the same time, the need for offices and housing contributed to steady growth in the construction industry. Today, thousands of banks and corporations have some connection to Delaware.

Workers take a lunch break on Market Street in Wilmington. Along with the rest of the country, Delaware faced tough economic times in 2010.

Challenging Times

In 2008, the U.S. economy took a major hit. Millions of Americans lost their jobs, and countless businesses folded. The hard economic times continued through 2009. The people of Delaware suffered along with the rest of the country. By the beginning of 2010, more than 38,000 people were out of work. Wilmington was hit the hardest. Nearly 13 percent of workers in the city were unemployed. The state's last two auto-manufacturing plants shut down. State employees were forced to take a pay cut. Governor Jack Markell praised the people of Delaware for remaining strong during the tough times. "I remain firmly convinced that our state's best days are ahead of us," he said.

The state flag is blue with Delaware's coat of arms (the image from the state seal) inside a buff-colored (yellowish) diamond. The date of Delaware's statehood is printed beneath the diamond.

Delaware's state seal includes the state's coat of arms in the center. The two men in the coat of arms are a farmer (to represent farming) and a militiaman (to represent liberty). The ox represents livestock, and corn and wheat represent agriculture. Water represents the Delaware River, and a ship represents shipbuilding and the coastal economy. Below these items is a banner with the state motto. Along the bottom of the seal are three years: 1704 is the year that Delaware's general assembly was established; 1776 is the year of American independence from Great Britain; and 1787 is Delaware's year of statehood.

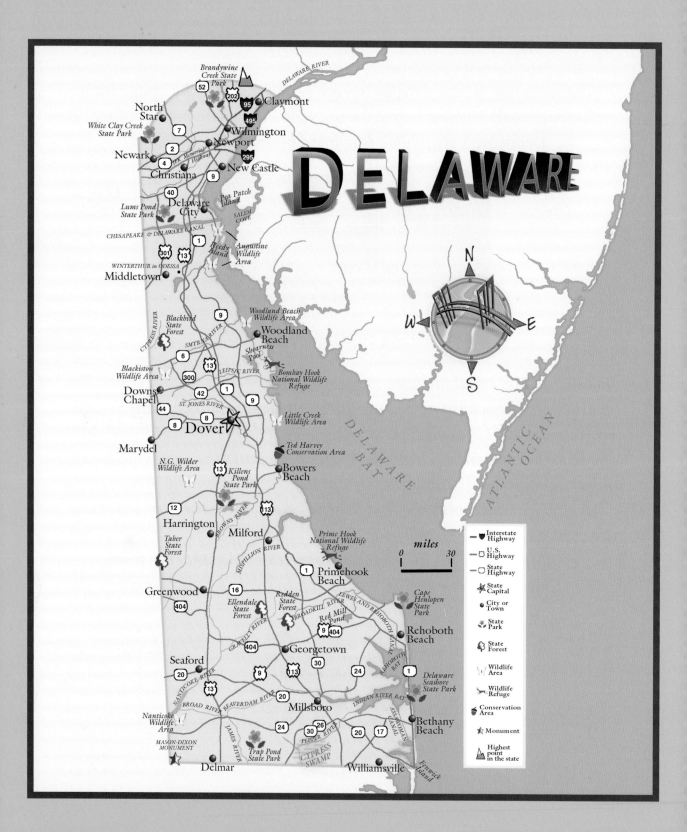

Brandywine
Creek State
Park

DELAWARE RIVER

52

202

95 Claymont

North
Star

495

White Clay Creek
State Park

7

Wilmington
Newport

2

295

Newark

4

KENNEDY MEMORIAL HIGHWAY

Christiana

9

New Castle

DELAWARE

40

Pea Patch
Island

Delaware
City

SALEM
COVE

Lums Pond
State Park

CHESAPEAKE & DELAWARE CANAL

301

1

Reedy
Island

Augustine
Wildlife
Area

WINTERTHUR in ODESSA

13

Middletown

CYPRESS RIVER

9

Woodland Beach
Wildlife Area

Blackbird
State
Forest

SMYRNA RIVER

Woodland
Beach

6

13

Shearness
Pool

LEIPSIC RIVER

Blackiston
Wildlife Area

300

Bombay Hook
National Wildlife
Refuge

Downs
Chapel

42

1

ST. JONES RIVER

9

44

Little Creek
Wildlife Area

8

Dover

8

Marydel

Ted Harvey
Conservation Area

N.G. Wilder
Wildlife Area

13

Killens
Pond
State Park

Bowers
Beach

BROWNS RIVER

12

113

Harrington

Milford

Taber
State
Forest

MISPILLION RIVER

Prime Hook
National Wildlife
Refuge

1

Primehook
Beach

Greenwood

16

404

Redden
State
Forest

BROADKILL RIVER

Ellendale
State
Forest

Cape
Henlopen
State
Park

LEWES AND REHOBOTH CANAL

Red Mill
Pond

9

404

GRAVELLY RIVER

Rehoboth
Beach

REHOBOTH BAY

Seaford

404

Georgetown

30

9

113

24

1

Delaware
Seashore
State Park

20

NANTICOKE RIVER

13

BEAVERDAM RIVER

20

Millsboro

INDIAN RIVER BAY

ASSAWOMAN CANAL

BROAD RIVER

Nanticoke
Wildlife
Area

JAMES RIVER

24

30

26

PEPPER RIVER

20

17

Bethany
Beach

MASON-DIXON
MONUMENT

Trap Pond
State Park

CYPRESS
SWAMP

Fenwick
Island

Delmar

Williamsville

DELAWARE
BAY

ATLANTIC
OCEAN

N

W   E

S

miles

0   30

Interstate
Highway

U.S.
Highway

State
Highway

State
Capital

City or
Town

State
Park

State
Forest

Wildlife
Area

Wildlife
Refuge

Conservation
Area

Monument

Highest
point
in the state

Our Delaware

words by George Hynson
music by William Brown

BOOKS

Bial, Raymond. *The Delaware*. New York: Marshall Cavendish Benchmark, 2005.

Giesecke, Ernestine. *State Government*. Chicago: Heinemann-Raintree, 2009.

Hossell, Karen. *Delaware, 1683–1776*. Washington, DC: National Geographic, 2006.

Iorio, Nicole. *Joe Biden*. Pleasantville, NY: Gareth Stevens, 2009.

WEBSITES

The Official Website for the First State:
http://www.delaware.gov

State of Delaware Kids Page:
http://www.delaware.gov/egov/portal.nsf/portal/kids

Visit Delaware:
http://www.visitdelaware.com

The White House Biography of Vice President Joe Biden:
http://www.whitehouse.gov/administration/vice-president-biden

David C. King is an award-winning author who has written more than forty books for children and young adults. He and his wife, Sharon, live in the Berkshires at the junction of New York, Massachusetts, and Connecticut. Their travels have taken them through most of the United States.

Brian Fitzgerald has been an editor and a writer of children's books for more than a decade. He lives in Connecticut with his wife and daughter. One of their favorite vacation spots is Rehoboth Beach.

★ INDEX ★

Page numbers in **boldface** are illustrations.